This book belongs to:
_____

I am _____ years old

My favourite colour is:
_____

Thank you for buying this book!

We hope that you enjoy An ABC of Thanks as much as we did in creating it! Please share it with anyone who you think would love it too, and as independent publishers, we really appreciate your reviews and feedback :)

Text copyright © Liza Miles
lizamiles.writer@gmail.com | www.lizamileswriter.com

Sign up to hear from Liza: https://mailchimp/342c8ea9ff10/liza-miles-writer

www.facebook.com/lizamileswriter   www.instagram.com/lizamileswriter

www.twitter.com/LOVEBIT28046864   www.tiktok.com/@lizamiles_writer

www.youtube.com/channel/UCqDeBqZp1BaSbKl1oclyb5g

Illustrations copyright © Melissa Royle-Guimarães
mj@mjroyle.com | www.mjroyle.com | www.justmjcreative.wixsite.com/mysite

Sign up to hear from Melissa: https://landing.mailerlite.com/webforms/landing/k0d9g4

www.facebook.com/mjroyle.author   www.instagram.com/m.j.royle.author

an ABC of thanks

Written by
Mary-Beth Mazzini

Illustrated by
Melissa Royle-Guimarães

Aa

Thank you for **apples** crunchy and sweet,
for **acorns**, from which oak trees grow.

Thank you for **art** and the fun that I have,
drawing houses and cats and rainbows.

Thank you for **angel** cake, **alphabet** soup,
ice cream, and strawberry sorbet.

Thank you for **animals**, wild ones and tame
and squirrels in the park where I play.

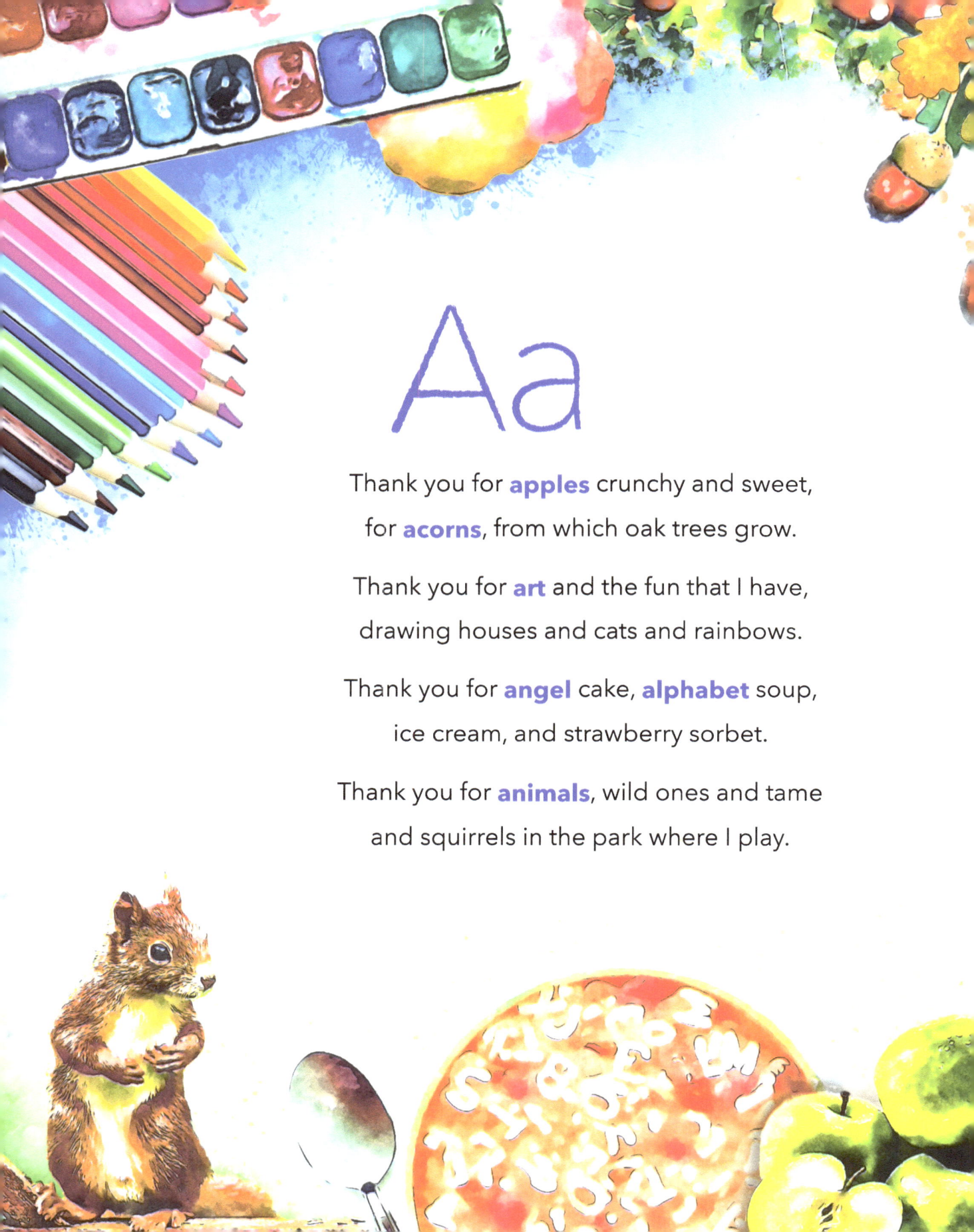

Bb

Thank you for **bees**, **busy** making honey,
for **baskets** woven with **bamboo**.

Thank you for **bathtime** in winter and summer,
water keeps me cosy, or cool.

Thank you for **bears**, who live in the wild,
for teddy who sleeps in my **bed**.

Thank you for **baking** my favourite cake
and letting me ice it **bright** red.

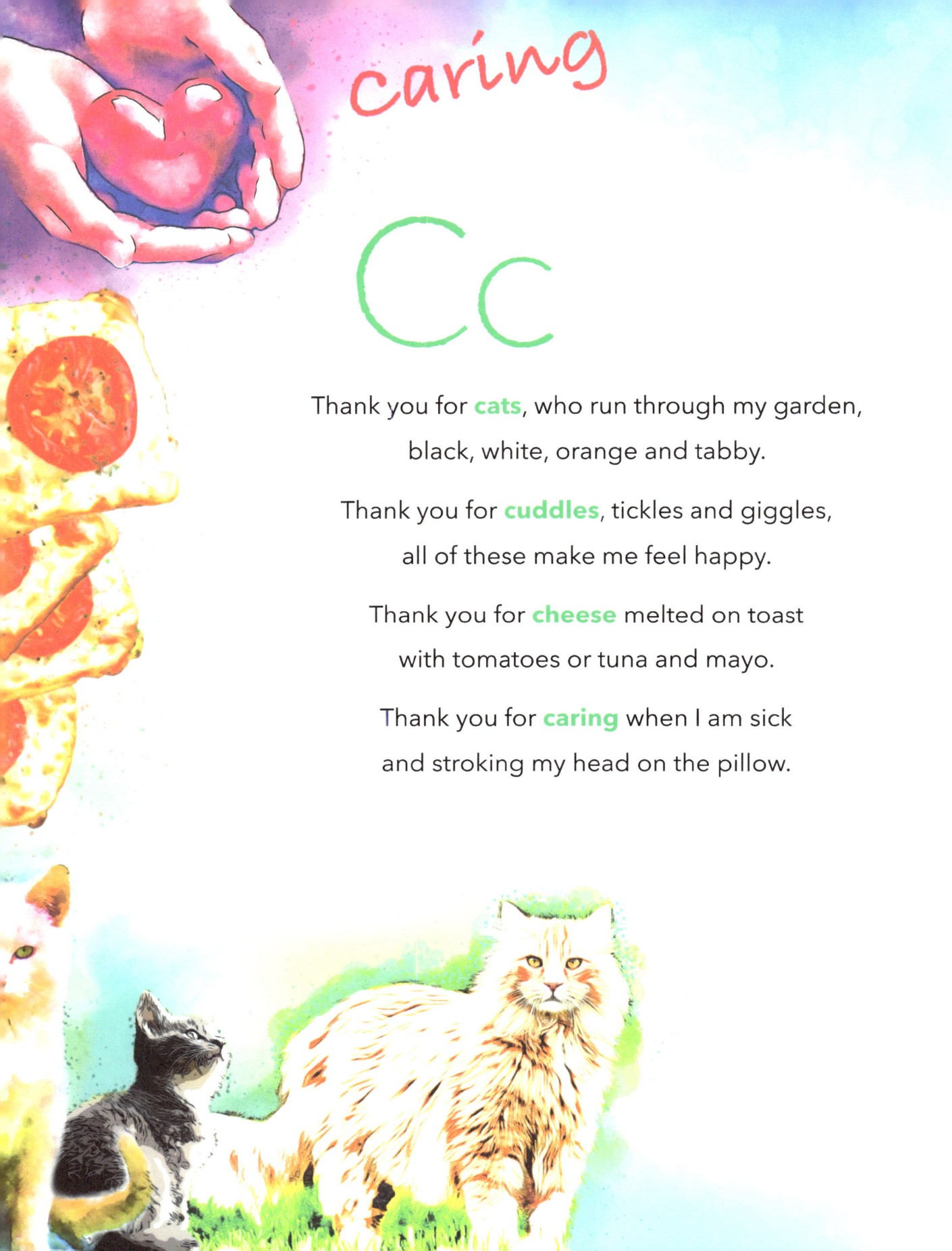

caring

Cc

Thank you for **cats**, who run through my garden,
black, white, orange and tabby.

Thank you for **cuddles**, tickles and giggles,
all of these make me feel happy.

Thank you for **cheese** melted on toast
with tomatoes or tuna and mayo.

Thank you for **caring** when I am sick
and stroking my head on the pillow.

Dd

Thank you for **dogs** who live near by,
chasing balls, wagging tails as they run.

Thank you for **drawing** pictures with me,
dressing up and imagining is fun.

Thank you for **dreams** I have in the night,
where I do things I can't in the **day**.

Thank you for **drums** I love the big noise,
Spanish **dancing** and shouting Olé!

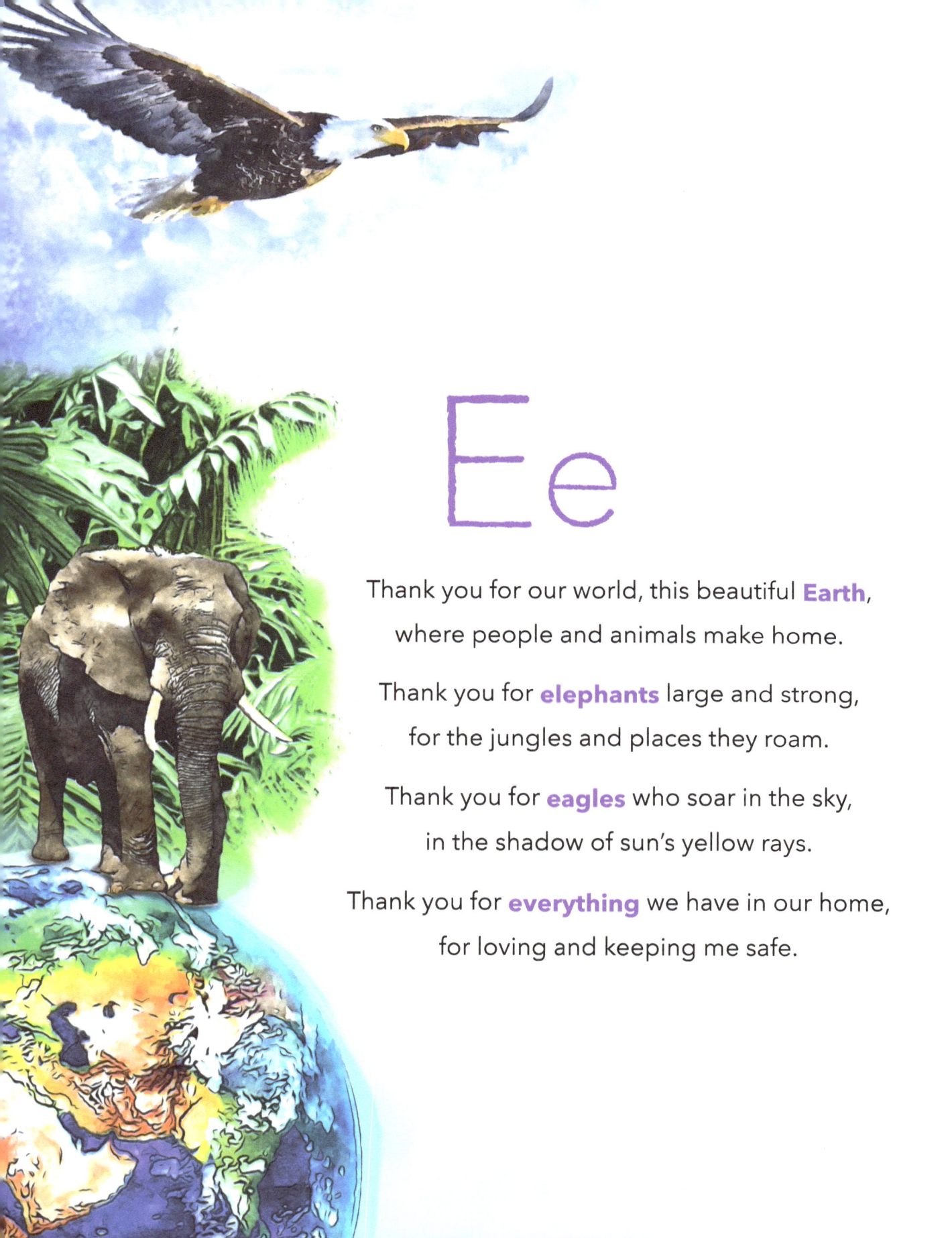

Ee

Thank you for our world, this beautiful **Earth**, where people and animals make home.

Thank you for **elephants** large and strong, for the jungles and places they roam.

Thank you for **eagles** who soar in the sky, in the shadow of sun's yellow rays.

Thank you for **everything** we have in our home, for loving and keeping me safe.

FUNNY FEET

Ff

Thank you for **friends**, we meet in the park,
for picnics and hiding behind trees.

Thank you for jokes and things which are **funny**,
for laughter when you tickle my **feet**.

Thank you for my **family**, for helping me grow
and showing me new things each day.

Thank you for **feelings**, from happy to cross
and **farmers** who feed animals with hay.

Gg

Thank you for fun days which make me yell **GREAT**!
When I'm swimming, or playing at the beach.

Thank you for **grass**, where I hop skip and play,
dewy softness soft under my feet.

Thank you for **giggling**, I love to laugh
and chuckle when you do something funny.

Thank you for **green** the colour of leaves,
giving snacks made from apples and honey.

Giving is Good!

Hh

Thank you for **hamsters**, small and furry,
for the pets we have in our **home**.

Thank you for **happy** times shared with my friends
and when I am playing alone.

Thank you for people, who work **helping** others
in **hospitals**, care **homes** and schools.

Thank you for **hats** I wear on my **head**
and the swim cap I wear in the pool.

I i

Thank you for **ink** used to print pictures,
and books that I like to read.

For **indigo** skies and **iridescent** colours,
for flowers grown from seed.

Thank you for **ice cream** which I love to lick,
for **icicles** which form when it's cold.

Thank you for **iguanas** who live in Brazil,
in America and North Mexico.

Jj

Thank you for **jam** which I spread on my toast
and for Gran who makes **jolly jam** tarts.

Thank you for **jelly** in red, blue or green,
which can be set into shapes, cubes or hearts.

Thank you for **jumping** on the trampoline,
I love leaping and bouncing up high.

Thank you for **jellyfish** who live in the sea
and for **jays** who fly high in the sky.

Jolly!

Kk

Thank you for **kites** that soar up above,
making patterns as they sail through the air.

Thank you for **knights** in stories of old -
who were brave and fought dragons in lairs.

Thank you for **kindness** from people, who know me,
for **kisses** and cuddles and hugs.

Thank you for **koalas** and **kangaroos**
who hang out in trees and eat shrubs.

Kindness

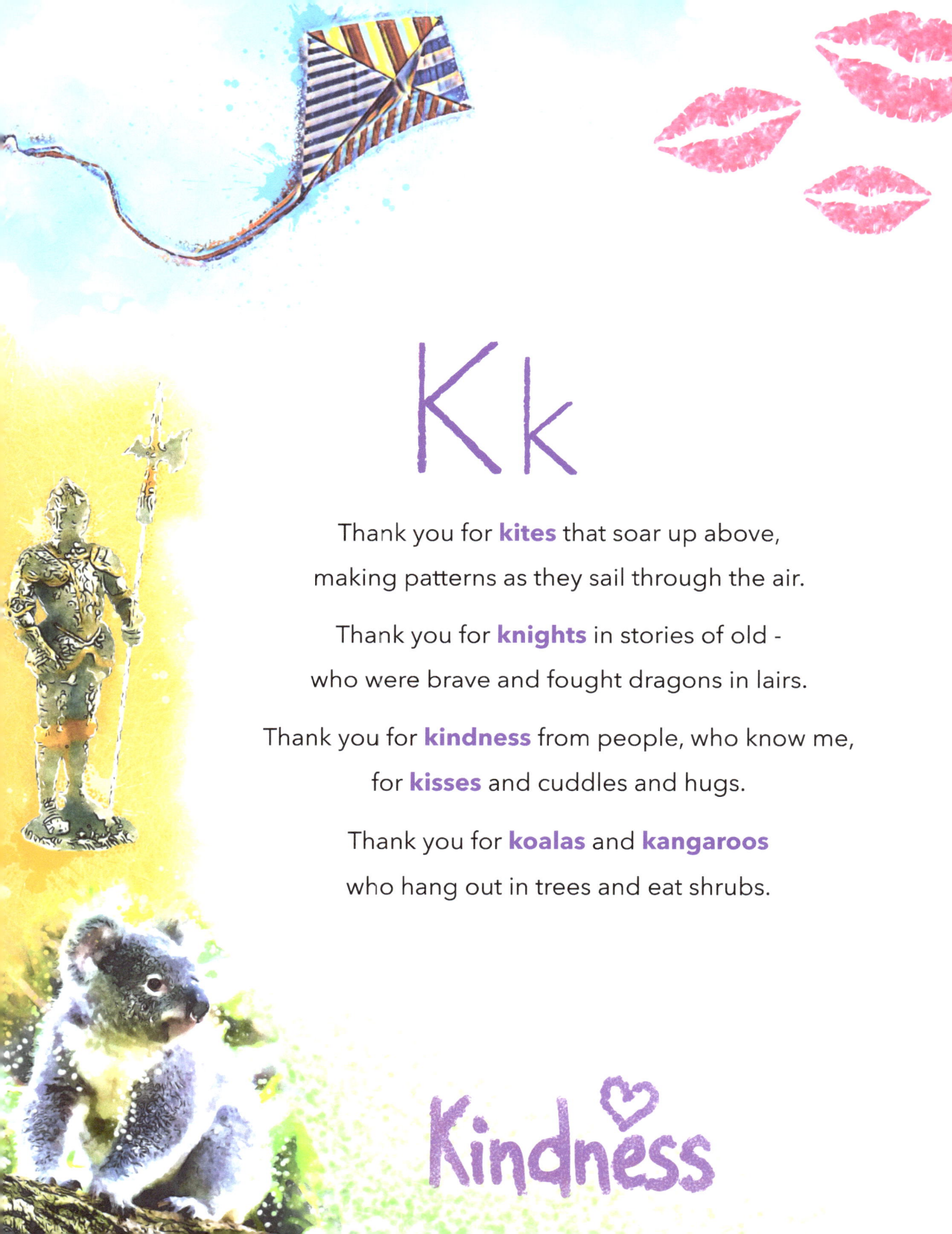

L l

Thank you for **little** which is me at the moment,
like an acorn, one day I'll grow.

For raindrops and sunshine and beaches and mountains,
with **large** peaks covered up in snow.

Thank you for **legs**, they help me to walk,
and run, skip or hop through the day.

Thank you for **laughing** softly and **loud**;
for **lavender** on the pillow where I **lay**.

Hehehe!
Teehee!
Hahaha!

Mm

Thank you for **mornings** when I get out of bed
and see the sun rise in the sky.

Thank you for **milk**, I enjoy with my lunch,
on porridge, or in custard with pie.

Thank you for **marmite**, spread on my bread,
cut in triangles, soldiers or squares.

Thank you for **marmalade**, sticky and sweet,
made from oranges, lemons or pears.

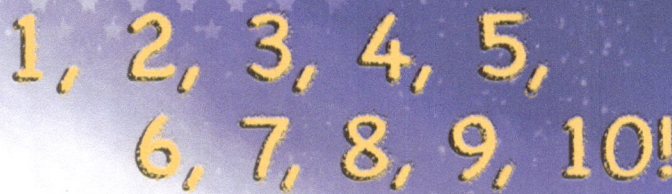

Nn

Thank you for **numbers** I can count one to ten,
I count on my fingers and toes.

Thank you for **nuts**, crunchy, salty or plain,
for **naps** or having a doze.

Thank you for **nurses** who work in the hospital,
for bedtime when stars twinkle bright.

Thank you for **newts** that turn into frogs,
for **nightingales** that sing through the **night**.

Oo

Thank you for **oranges**, round, juicy and sweet, growing on trees in the sun.

Thank you for **old** like the stories you tell about things you did when you were young.

Thank you for **otters**, who scamper on banks, and swim in fresh water, so clean.

Thank you for **orchestras**, who play beautiful music in theatres and parks and on the screen.

Pp

Thank you for **people** from all round the world whose lives are so different from my own.

Thank you for **places** on maps in my school, like Africa, Egypt and Rome.

Thank you for **penguins**, who live in Antarctic, they can walk many miles in one day.

Thank you for **porpoises** who live in cold water in fjords and harbours and bays.

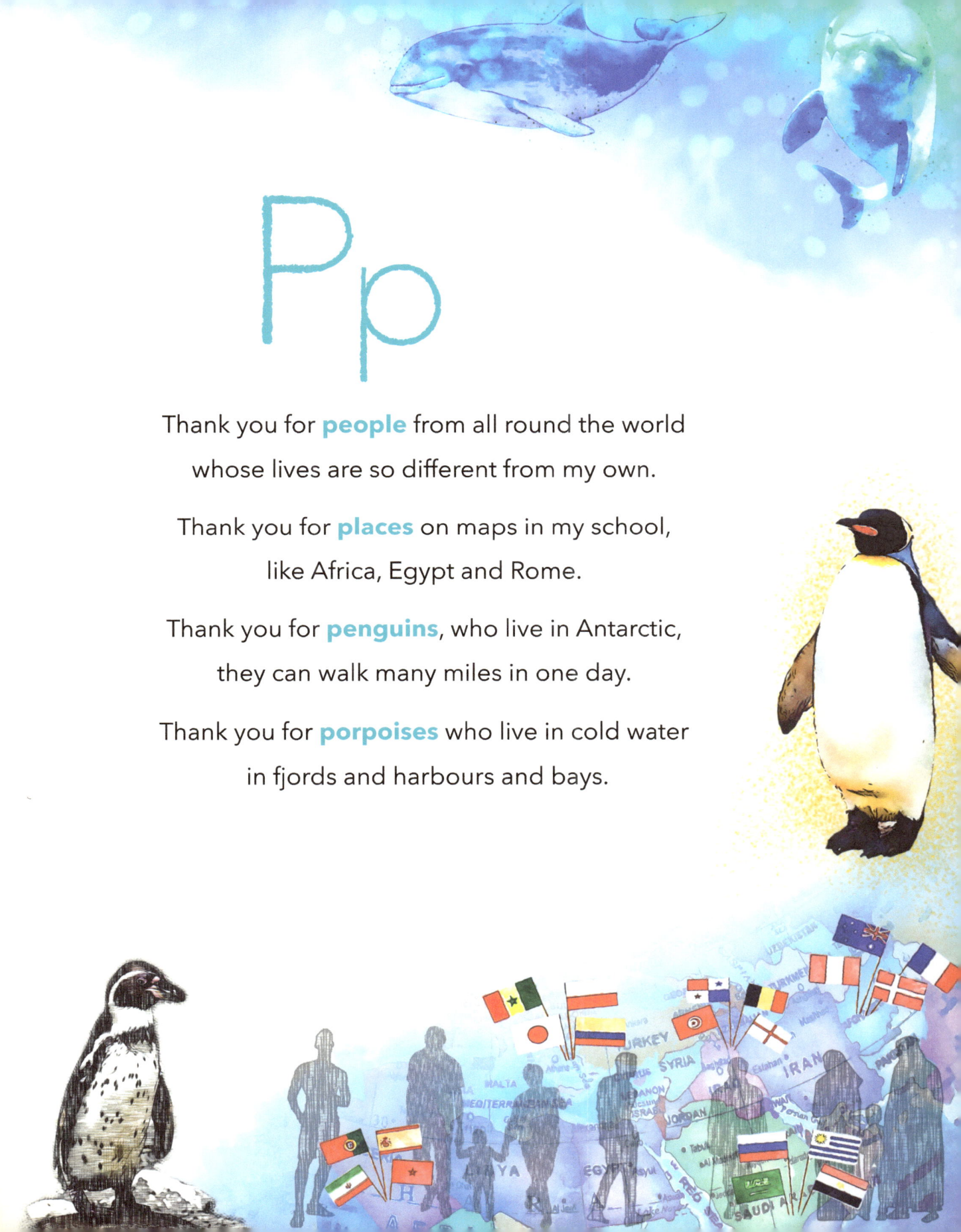

Qq

Thank you for **questions** which help me to learn,
I can ask my family and teachers.

Thank you for **quizzes** and Fairytale **Queens**,
who rule over lands and strange creatures.

Thank you for **quails** who live in the meadow,
and for ducks who **quack** when they roam.

Thank you for **quesadillas** cut into **quarters**
and for **quiet** times, together in our home.

Quack Quack!

Rr

Thank you for **rain**, which falls in the rivers, giving water for food and for drinking.

Thank you for **rabbits** that live in the wild and tame ones whose fur I like stroking.

Thank you for **running**, running is fun, playing chase, and **riding** on a bike.

Thank you for **rainbows**, after the rain, for **roaming** the hills on a hike.

Ss

Thank you for **shortbread** my favourite biscuit,
it's a crumbly, buttery treat.

Thank you for **Scotland**, her mountains and glens,
covered in heather, bracken and peat.

Thank you for **sand**, so golden and **soft**,
it **sparkles** when lit by **sun's** rays.

Thank you for **swallows** who **soar** through the air
and **swans** who glide with such grace.

Tt

Thank you for **toads**, big spotty and brown,
and **tadpoles** who swim under logs.

Thank you for mammals, **tiny** insects **too**
whose homes are in marshes and bogs.

Thank you for **toast**, covered in butter
or floating on **top** of my soup.

Thank you for **time** you spend with me
and for **taking** me places with you.

Uu

Thank you for **umbrellas** they help keep me dry and shade me from the sun at the beach.

Thank you for planes, which fly in the sky, high **up**, and far out of reach.

Thank you for **unicorns** a magical beast, for **ukuleles** and lullabies at night.

Thank you for **understanding**, when I am sad, or frightened, because something is not right.

understanding 💜

Vv

Thank you for **vacations**, imagined and real
for **views** in stories and books.

Thank you for **violins**, pianos and trumpets,
and **violas** and whistles and flutes.

Thank you for **vines** of dark grapes and flowers,
their blooms make a **vivid** display.

Thank you for **vegetables** you cook for my dinner,
you make sure I eat up five everyday!

Ww

Thank you for **white**, soft crunchy snow,
my footprints leave tracks where I've been.

Thank you for the **weeping willow** tree,
with tendrils of soft yellow green.

Thank you for **winter**, and outdoor games,
I can ski or ride fast on a sleigh.

Thank you for **worms** who help the soil breathe,
and keep it clean, as they burrow away.

With lots of love
x x x x x

Xx

Thank you for **X**, the twenty fourth letter,
a kiss sign for Daddy or Mummy.

Thank you for games using **X's** and O's,
when you lose you make a face that is funny.

Thank you for **x-ray** it helps doctors to know
when a bone is not set the right way.

Thank you for **xylophones**, they make a nice sound,
they tinkle loud or soft when I play.

Yippee!

Yy

Thank you for **yellow**, the colour of Sun,
of roses and daffodils too.

Thank you for **yippee**, which I **yell** when I'm happy,
and when some of my wishes come true.

Thank you for **yams**, orange and sweet,
for the **yogurts** you give me for fuel.

Thank you for **yaks** from faraway places
like Mongolia, China and Nepal.

Zigzag

Z z

Thank you for **zebra**, black and white striped, related to horses and donkeys.

Thank you for **zeros** and counting to ten like in games of ten little monkeys.

Thank you for **zigzag** it's fun to skip or walk going sideways to side.

Thank you for **zips** like the ones on my coat that keeps me all cosy and dry.

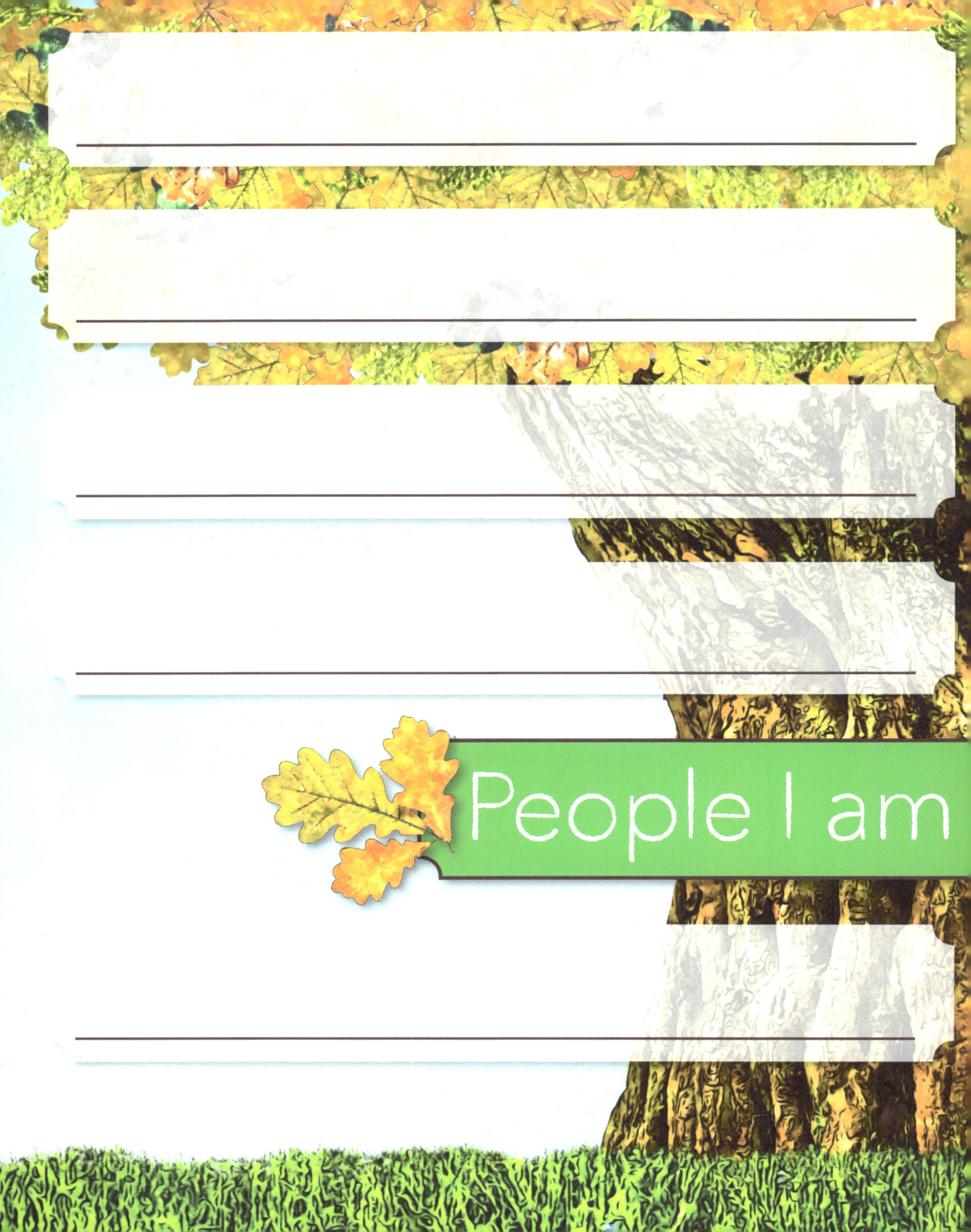